NBA Champions: Philadelphia 76ers

Forward Chet Walker

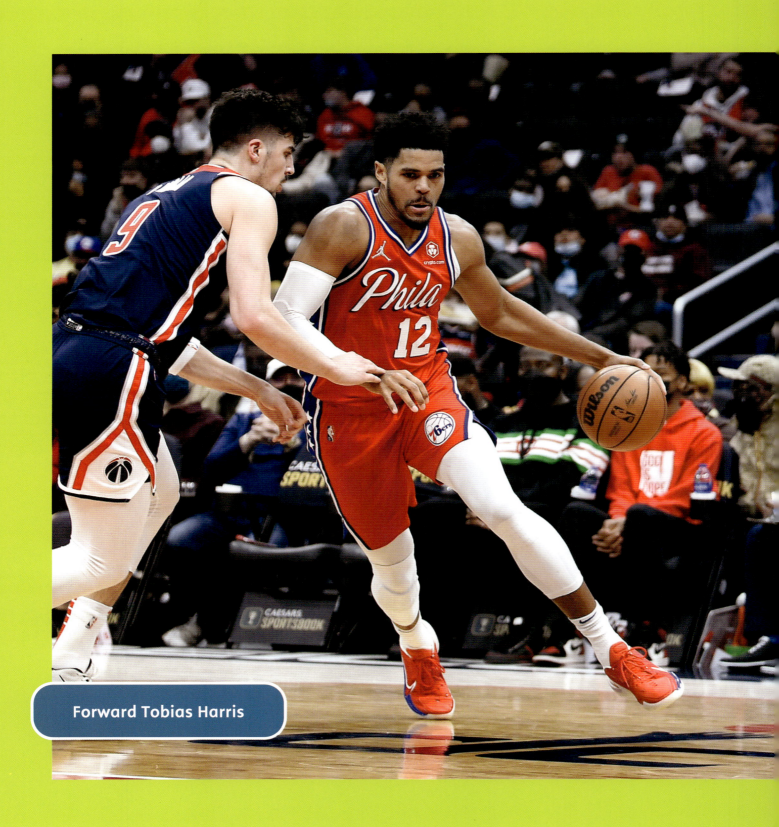

Forward Tobias Harris

NBA CHAMPIONS

PHILADELPHIA 76ERS

DENNY BULCAO, JR.

CREATIVE EDUCATION / CREATIVE PAPERBACKS

Forward Julius Erving

Published by Creative Education and Creative Paperbacks
P.O. Box 227, Mankato, Minnesota 56002
Creative Education and Creative Paperbacks are imprints of
The Creative Company
www.thecreativecompany.us

Art Direction by Tom Morgan
Book production by Graham Morgan
Edited by Grace Cain

Images by Getty Images/Bettmann, 4, Focus On Sport, 1, 3, 6, 19, 24, G Fiume, 2, John G. Zimmerman, 12, Manny Millan, 16, Mitchell Leff, cover, 5, 10, Neil Leifer, cover, 7, Sarah Stier, 20, Walter Iooss Jr., 15; Pexels/Trev Adams, 9

Every effort has been made to contact copyright holders for material reproduced in this book. Any omissions will be rectified in subsequent printings if notice is given to the publisher.

Copyright © 2025 Creative Education, Creative Paperbacks
International copyright reserved in all countries. No part of this book may be reproduced in any form without written permission from the publisher.

Library of Congress Cataloging-in-Publication Data
Names: Bulcao, Denny Jr., author.
Title: Philadelphia 76ers / by Denny Bulcao Jr..
Description: Mankato, Minnesota : Creative Education and Creative Paperbacks, [2025] | Series: Creative sports: nba champions | Includes index. | Audience: Ages 7-10 | Audience: Grades 2-3 | Summary: "Elementary-level text and dynamic sports photos highlight the NBA championship wins of the Philadelphia 76ers, plus sensational players associated with the professional basketball team such as Joel Embiid"— Provided by publisher.
Identifiers: LCCN 2024014036 (print) | LCCN 2024014037 (ebook) | ISBN 9798889892632 (library binding) | ISBN 9781682776292 (paperback) | ISBN 9798889893745 (ebook)
Subjects: LCSH: Philadelphia 76ers (Basketball team)—History—Juvenile literature. | Basketball players—United States—Juvenile literature.
Classification: LCC GV885.52.P45 B85 2025 (print) | LCC GV885.52.P45 (ebook) | DDC 796.323/64—dc23/eng/20240404
LC record available at https://lccn.loc.gov/2024014036
LC ebook record available at https://lccn.loc.gov/2024014037

Printed in China

Center Joel Embiid

Forward Charles Barkley

CONTENTS

Home of the 76ers	8
Naming the 76ers	13
76ers History	14
Other 76ers Stars	18
About the 76ers	22
Glossary	23
Index	24

Home of the 76ers

Philadelphia is Pennsylvania's largest city. It is known for its history surrounding the birth of our country. The Declaration of Independence and the Constitution were both signed in this city. Philadelphia has an **arena** called the Wells Fargo Center. It is home to the 76ers basketball team.

NBA CHAMPIONS

Center Joel Embiid

he Philadelphia 76ers are a National Basketball Association (NBA) team. They compete in the Atlantic Division. That's part of the Eastern Conference. Their **rivals** are the New York Knicks and Boston Celtics. All NBA teams want to win the **NBA Finals** and become champions.

Center Wilt Chamberlain

Naming the 76ers

The team began as the Syracuse Nationals in 1946. They became the 76ers when they moved to Philadelphia in 1963. The Founding Fathers voted to make the United States a new country in 1776.

76ers History

The Syracuse Nationals were part of the National Basketball League before joining the NBA in 1949. The team's best player was tough forward Dolph Schayes. He made the All-Star team 12 times! He led the Nationals to their first NBA championship in 1955.

After becoming the 76ers, the team won its second championship in 1967. Philly fans loved watching forward Billy Cunningham leap for rebounds. They called him "The Kangaroo Kid."

Forward Billy Cunningham

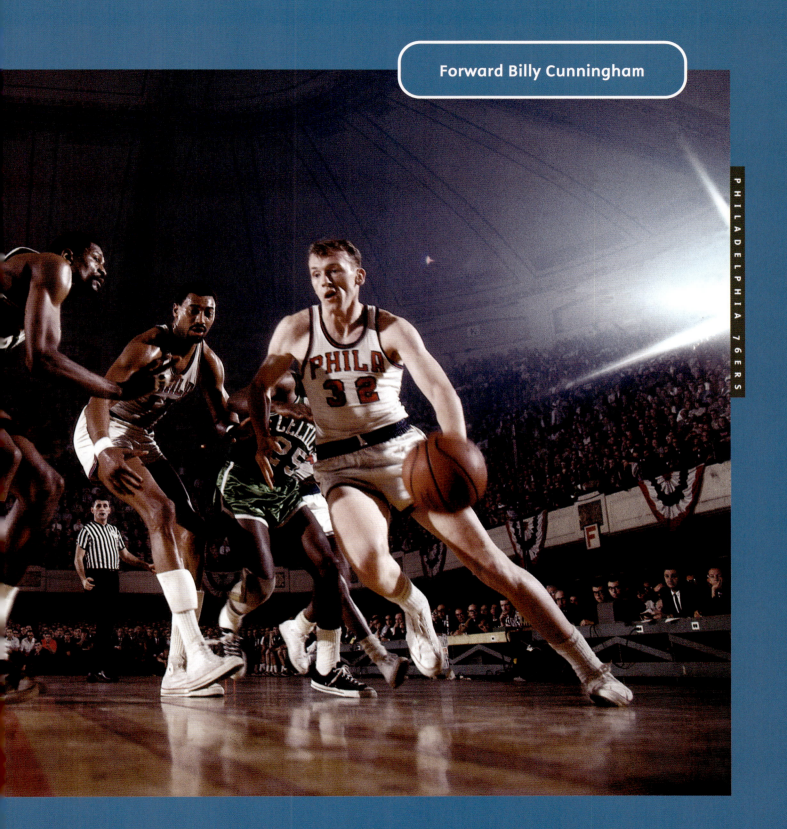

PHILADELPHIA 76ERS

NBA CHAMPIONS

Center Moses Malone

16

The 76ers won 65 games in the 1982–83 season and won a third **title**. Other teams could not stop powerful center Moses Malone or high-jumping forward Julius Erving. Erving was nicknamed "Dr. J." He won one NBA **Most Valuable Player (MVP)** award. He was also an 11-time All-Star.

The 76ers reached the Finals again in 2001. They did not win the title. Speedy guard Allen Iverson excited Philly fans with his quick moves. "A.I." was inducted into the Basketball Hall of Fame in 2016.

Other 76ers Stars

The 76ers have had many stars. Guard Hal Greer was one of the team's best scorers for 15 seasons. Greer and 7-foot-1 center Wilt Chamberlain were key players during the 1966–67 championship season. Chamberlain won three of his four NBA Most Valuable Player awards with the 76ers.

Point guard Maurice "Mo" Cheeks was a very good passer and defender. Forward Charles Barkley was a tough player. He was not very tall, but he was a great rebounder.

Guard Hal Greer

NBA CHAMPIONS

Guard Tyrese Maxey

Center Joel Embiid joined the 76ers for the 2016–17 season. He stands a whopping 7 feet tall! Embiid has won many awards. He was named the NBA's Most Valuable Player for the 2022–23 season. Fans are hopeful for a fourth championship!

About the 76ers

First season: 1946–47

Conference/division: Eastern Conference, Atlantic Division

Team colors: blue, red, navy, silver, and white

Home arena: Wells Fargo Center

NBA CHAMPIONSHIPS:

1955, 4 games to 3 over Fort Wayne Pistons

1967, 4 games to 2 over San Francisco Warriors

1983, 4 games to 0 over Los Angeles Lakers

TEAM WEBSITE:

https://www.nba.com/sixers/

Glossary

arena — a large building with seats for spectators, where sports games and entertainment events are held

Most Valuable Player (MVP) — an honor given to the season's best player

NBA Finals — a series of games between two teams at the end of the playoffs; the first team to win four games is the champion

rival — a team that plays extra hard against another team

title — another word for championship

Forward Julius Erving

NBA CHAMPIONS

Index

Barkley, Charles, 6, 18

Chamberlain, Wilt, 12, 18

Cheeks, Maurice "Mo", 18

Cunningham, Billy, 14, 15

Embiid, Joel, 5, 10, 21

Erving, Julius, 4, 17

Greer, Hal, 18, 19

Iverson, Allen, 17

Malone, Moses, 16, 17

Schayes, Dolph, 14

team name, 13, 14

Wells Fargo Center, 8, 22